Tutor Your Way to Money & Fun: The Only Tutoring Guide You'll Ever Need

Make $25 to $150 an hour and more!

Tutor Dominus

CONTENTS

"Instant access to anything is the future. So if you need a tutor or a baby sitter or a massage or any service, it's going to be instantly available, 24 hours a day, through your phone, with one click."
~ Jason Calacanis, Startup Entrepreneur

"Do not train a child to learn by force or harshness; but direct them to it by what amuses their minds, so that you may be better able to discover with accuracy the peculiar bent of the genius of each."
~ Plato

.

1

SEVEN REASONS FOR BECOMING A TUTOR

Tutoring is a highly rewarding profession, and not just monetarily. Tutors actually perform a benefit to society, helping kids get ahead in school. With tutoring, young people become more knowledgeable, they are better educated, and they end up learning how to study better.

By the way, it isn't just kids who benefit from tutoring; many adults have utilized the services of tutors also. More on that in a later chapter.

Here are seven reasons why you should consider becoming a tutor:

1. Generate a high income. For some tutors, earnings of $25 to $35 an hour are common. Some tutors of more specialized topics can make $150 an hour or more.
2. Can be done part-time or full time. It's up to you how many hours you put into it, and whether you want to turn tutoring into a full time job.

3. Make your own hours. You can decide when you want to work. If you have another job and just want to tutor weekends, that's fine. You want to keep your weekends free? No problem, just work afternoons and evenings on weekdays.

4. You are helping kids. You are actually providing an important benefit to young people. One tutor has described it as doing community service and getting paid for it.

5. Set your own work location. You want to work out of your house? That's fine. You want to work at your clients house? That's fine also. Or maybe you just want to work in the study rooms at libraries. More on that later. You get to decide where you want to work and how far you want to drive.

6. Be your own boss. If you don't care for working for someone else, then being a tutor is the way to go, since you report to no one but your self.

7. Putting your skills to work. Why waste your skills and knowledge? If you are good at math and/or English, why not pass those skills along? From a mental standpoint, it helps you also.

So what do I know about tutoring and teaching? I am a former teacher and have tutored all age groups for several years. Hopefully, I can pass my knowledge about tutoring on to you through this book.

2

ARE YOU A TUTOR?

Many people who have considered tutoring are wondering if they can really do it. Especially if they haven't had any "real teaching experience". So what is teaching experience?

Have you ever helped other students study for a test when you were in college? Have you ever coached one of your kid's soccer teams? Were you ever the leader of a club that you are a member of? Have you ever had to give a presentation at work? Have you ever had to train a new staff member as part of your job? Have you ever helped a neighbor with a computer problem? Have you ever helped your own child with his or her homework?

If your answer to any of these questions is "yes" then you have had real life teaching experience. These are all examples of teaching and tutoring.

If you are a patient person and you have a lot of knowledge in one or more educational areas and you can explain those concepts in a simple and understandable format, then you can be a tutor.

3

WHAT CAN YOU TEACH?

It is OK to specialize, but don't narrow your focus. If you are great at English, but are able to help a child with third grade math, then why not add third grade math to your repertoire.

If you know a lot about science, then tutoring high school students for ACT or SAT preparation would be appropriate.

Some tutors specialize in an age group, such as only high school students or only elementary students. However, opening your horizons to additional grades or ages will expand your market and increase your income.

As one example, I have a friend who tutors both a kindergarten girl, a high school junior, and a 35 year old businessman. Don't limit your options.

Here are some of the subjects that tutors provide tutoring for:

English
Vocabulary
Grammar

Reading
Handwriting & Penmanship
Adding
Subtracting
Multiplying
Dividing
Algebra I
Algebra II
Pre-Algebra
Geometry
Trigonometry
Pre-Calculus
Calculus
Statistics
Discrete Math
Middle Grades Math
Chemistry
Physics
Biology
Earth Science
Anatomy & Physiology
Elementary Science
Middle School Science
Essay Writing
Literature
U.S. History
World History
Elementary Social Studies
Middle School Social Studies
High School Social Studies
Advanced Placement Calculus AB
Advanced Placement Calculus BC
Advanced Placement Statistics

Advanced Placement Biology
Advanced Placement Chemistry
Advanced Placement Physics B
Advanced Placement English Language
Advanced Placement English Literature
Advanced Placement U.S. History
Advanced Placement World History
Advanced Placement European History
Advanced Placement Government and Politics

ACT English
ACT Mathematics
ACT Reading
ACT Science
ACT Writing

SAT Prep English Literature
SAT Prep U.S. History
SAT Prep World History
SAT Prep Mathematics Level 1
SAT Prep Mathematics Level 2
SAT Prep Biology
SAT Prep Chemistry
SAT Prep Physics

Don't forget the "Think Outside the Box" subjects. For example:
Cooking
Gardening
Website Design
Coding
Organizing
Car Repair

Resume Writing
Dancing
Fitness
Nutrition
Piano Playing
Guitar Playing
Parenting
Drawing
Painting
Floral Design
Sewing
Stock Trading
Real Estate Investing
Tai Chi
Yoga
Creative Writing
Genealogy
Woodworking
Small Business Development
Microsoft Office
Microsoft Word
Microsoft Excel
Microsoft PowerPoint
Microsoft Outlook
Microsoft Windows 10
QuickBooks
Foreign Languages (Spanish, French, Chinese, etc.)

.

4 AN AGENCY OR ON YOUR OWN?

There are actually three ways to work as a tutor: working as an employee for a large tutoring organization, working as an independent contractor through an agency, or working for yourself.

Working for a large tutor company is the lowest paying option. According to payscale.com, the average tutor employee makes $17.28 per hour. Glassdoor.com has a listing of the average wage for tutors broken down by company. The amounts range from $9.28 to $21.08 per hour.

The large companies are fairly well known, such as Sylvan Learning Centers, Huntington Learning Centers, and Kumon Group. Starting with these companies may be a good way to get your feet wet, but your earnings will be far lower than the other alternatives.

Registering with an agency is a good option, especially when starting out. The primary reason is that they find the clients for you. If you go to a search engine and type in tutors, you will find a wide range of tutoring agencies. Scroll down to the bottom of the home pages and look for a link that says "Careers" or "Tutoring Jobs". The hourly pay will be higher than what the large companies pay their employees, but less than what you could make on your own. The way it works is, as an example, the agency may charge the client $50 an hour and pay you $35 an hour.

Finally, you can work for yourself, charging what the agencies and large companies charge, and keeping it all for yourself. The biggest disadvantage of course, is that you have to find your own clients. If you can overcome that hurdle, then you have it made.

5

WHERE SHOULD YOU TUTOR?

In regards to locations to do the tutoring, you have at least three choices: your home, their home, or the library. These are the three main ones but there are actually a few other options, such as Starbucks (yes, I've tutored at Starbucks) and the child's school.

I have found that the most comfortable and study-appropriate place to tutor is the local public library. Most libraries have study rooms, and the few that don't usually have several tables that are appropriate for tutoring if you keep your voices low.

Libraries are generally convenient and "neutral ground." Plus, they are away from distractions that a child might find in his or her home.

Unfortunately, the demand for study rooms has increased significantly over the years, requiring patrons to sign up ahead of time to get a time slot for use of one of the rooms. But once you are in the study room, it is quiet and a scholarly atmosphere is created.

Personally, I never tutor at my home, for various

reasons. I leave it up to the client regarding whether they would prefer to have me to come to their home or meet at the library.

One other option is tutoring remotely, utilizing a service such as Skype, but this will be covered in a later chapter.

6

SHOULD YOU LOOK AT YOUR CELL PHONE
WHEN TUTORING?

The simple answer is "No."

Don't take phone calls, don't text, don't check your emails, and don't go on Facebook. Your time during the tutoring session should be totally dedicated to your student.

The only exception might be if you are expecting an extremely important phone call, such as a relative who is pregnant and expecting a baby any minute. In that case, you need to inform the parent of the student ahead of time that you may be getting an important call and let them know why.

There may be certain circumstances when working with a student, where you need to look up the spelling or definition of a word. In that case, if it is related specifically to the tutoring, then checking this information on a cell phone would be OK.

The one other time (no pun intended) you may need to check your phone is to see what time it is. If there is no clock in the room, and you want to keep to a schedule, wait until you think that there is only five or ten minutes left in the session, then check your phone quickly to see the time.

7

HOW LONG SHOULD THE TUTORING SESSION LAST?

Most tutoring sessions last one hour, but I have tutored half hour sessions and one-and-a-half hour sessions. Once you get beyond an hour and a half, the student starts to become antsy, whether the student is a first grader or a twelfth grader, or even an adult.

My advice is to leave it up to the client. One thing to consider is your travelling distance. If you have to drive a long way to the client's house, you don't want to make it a half hour or 45 minute session. You need to make it worth your while. In that case, you can tell the client that your sessions are a one hour minimum.

8

WHEN IS IT OK TO YELL AT A CHILD?

The short answer is "never." However, I did yell at a third grader once, and it was justified. More about that in a minute.

But first, I want to remind you that you are not the student's parent; you're not even the student's babysitter.

Obviously, you will deal with students who are over-active if you work with those in elementary school, who like to play with their pencils and erasers, and all you have to do is tell them to stay on task.

If the attention deficit of the student is extreme, talk to the parent about it. Don't yell. I actually tutored a student who told me that his previous tutor would yell at him constantly, and how he hated being hollered at.

If there are disciplinary issues that need to take place, report it to the parent, and let them deal with it.

Now back to the one time that I yelled. I tutored a seven year old boy who was a bit hyperactive, but it never got to me. However, one time, he wanted to get something from another room. He had scissors in both hands, not kid scissors but grown-up scissors, with the blades opened wide. He started running out of the room.

I immediately yelled, "Stop! Don't ever run with scissors in your hands!" I then instructed him on the appropriate way of holding scissors while walking. This was the one time when shouting at a student was justified.

9

DON'T TOUCH THAT CHILD

It seems like it shouldn't even be necessary to mention this but it is important. There is no reason to touch a child in a tutoring session for any reason. There shouldn't be any hint of impropriety.

Don't ever pat a child on the head. It is considered inappropriate and rude in numerous cultures including India, Thailand, and Laos. (Did you see the *Gran Torino* movie?)

Often, a high school student will offer to shake hands. That is OK.

10

WHY TUTORS NEED TO WEAR NEW SOCKS

Speaking of different cultures, one of the things I noticed going to various clients and houses, is that many families ask me to remove my shoes at the front door.

This practice was not limited to particular cultures or ethnic groups. I experienced this with a Hispanic family, an Indian family, and a white Anglo family.

The custom of removing shoes before entering a home is common throughout Asian countries. But this practice isn't limited to just people from Asian countries. The practice is common in such places as Turkey, Sweden, Germany, and Switzerland, and even in the State of Hawaii.

So the point I'm trying to make is, be prepared. Make sure your socks are clean, and don't have holes or show sign of wear. You never know when you have to show your socks to others.

11

WHAT TO WEAR

Speaking of socks, let's talk about the rest of your apparel. When you meet a client in person for the first time, you will want to set a good impression. That includes dressing appropriately and professionally.

What that means is no blue jeans or denims, no T-shirts, and no athletic shoes. Imagine you are going on an interview for the first time, because that is what is really happening.

Men don't necessarily have to wear a suit and tie but a dress shirt, khakis, and leather shoes would be appropriate. Women don't have to wear a dress but a blouse and women's dress pants would be fine.

Moving to slightly more casual attire might be OK if you have worked with the client for a long time, but keep in mind, the client looks at you as a professional.

This would apply if you are meeting with the mother and/or father of the child you are tutoring, or an adult being tutored.

There is one exception to this. If you are a college student tutoring another college student, you can get away with the college student appearance. In other words, you don't have to dress like a professor, although it wouldn't be a bad thing if you did. College students being tutored are more open to a casually dressed tutor.

One other point that needs to be mentioned if you do any online tutoring. You may have a tendency to dress more casually since the student usually just sees your face. Just make sure that you aren't wearing a T-shirt with inappropriate words or pictures.

I still recommend dressing as you would if you were seeing the student in person. You never know when you might have to jump out of your seat for some reason, while you are still online and visible to the student.

12

BABY SITTING – NOT!

If you are tutoring elementary or middle school students, I strongly recommend that you have a policy that the parent must be there during the entire session, not necessarily in the same room but close by. This would be whether you are teaching at the client's house or the library. As I stated previously, you are not a baby sitting service.

Here is an example of a situation you would not want to get into. You are tutoring a second grade girl at the library. The mother tells you that she needs to run to the store and will be back in a couple minutes. Your session is now over and the mother hasn't returned yet. You are supposed to leave right away to get to your next tutoring appointment. What do you do? Do you wait with the girl until her mother comes back, then show up late for your next appointment? Do you leave and let the girl fend for herself? Do you report the issue to the librarian? Who is responsible if you leave and something happens to the girl?

The same situation could happen if you are teaching a child at her house, except that there is no librarian that you can pass the responsibility to.

This may never happen to you, but you really don't want to be put in this position if it ever does.

How about this for solving the problem? Don't let it happen in the first place.

13

HOW MUCH MONEY YOU CAN MAKE

Deciding what to charge for tutoring may sound like a difficult decision, but it is actually fairly simple. There are several web sites where you can check on the going rate for tutors.

If you are working through an agency, the amount of your pay may be set, but there may be a little leeway for negotiation. Remember, that they have already quoted an hourly rate to the client, and they have to take a cut.

However, if you are dealing directly with a client in terms of payment, you can basically set your rate to whatever you want. You don't want to price yourself out of the market, but you also don't want to sell yourself too cheap.

You can check various web sites, CraigsList ads, and other sources to see what tutors are charging in your area for the topics you are interested in teaching.

One of the best web sites with this type of information is findtutorsnearme.com, which has a menu at the top right called Tutor Rates. Click on it and it will bring you to a page with all the states in the United States. Click on your state and scroll down past the maps until you get to the cities in your state. It gives the average tutoring rate for each city, which should provide you with a great guideline. (By the way, I have no connection to this web site. I just think it is a great resource.)

14

HOW TO CHARGE

The tutoring agencies usually charge by a set of hours upfront, such as a five hour package, a ten hour, and a twenty hours, with a greater discount per hour the more hours purchased up front.

If you are charging directly to a client, you could do that also (I do it with one client), but usually clients prefer to pay after each session.

By the way, I strongly recommend that you collect the fee right after the tutoring session. You don't want to get into a situation where the client says, "Oh, can I just pay you for both sessions next week?"

The common ways to be paid are by cash, check, and Paypal. I've been paid with checks by clients for a long time, and have never had a problem. Usually a client who wants their child tutored is generally very responsible from a financial standpoint.

When I first talk to a client, I tell them that either cash or check is fine, payable after each session.

Tutor Dominus

15 CHECKLIST

Before you get started with a new client, you should go over a list of items with them letting them know what the guidelines and expectations are. It doesn't have to be provided to them in a formal printed or emailed document, it can be discussed over-the-phone or in person in a conversational way.

Here is what should be covered:

1. What the child should bring to each session
    a. Pencils with erasers
    b. Paper (pad, notebook, or loose paper)
    c. Any homework that needs to be covered
    d. Any books that need to be covered
2. How much you charge, and when payment is due
3. What you do in the event of a no show (more about that in another chapter)
4. How often, what days, and what time of day for the sessions
5. Contact information, both yours and theirs
    a. Phone number
    b. Email
6. Smoking issues

a. I'm not exactly sure how to address this and I've only run into it once. I am actually allergic to tobacco smoke, and I had one client who vaped instead of smoked while I was tutoring her child in the next room, but for some reason, I could still smell it. It wasn't as strong as a regular cigarette, so it didn't bother me that much, but if it did, I probably would have asked her to refrain while I am there.

7. When notification of a session cancellation needs to be made

a. What happens if you show up and they aren't there, or they give you a very short notification of cancellation

16

NO SHOWS COST YOU MONEY

One of the most irritating issues that can happen is to drive 45 minutes to a tutoring session, then discover no one is home. This has actually happened to me a couple times. I knocked on the door, and tried calling the client but no answer. We eventually settled on a fee of 50% of what I normally charge for the hour.

The tutoring agencies usually have a policy of charging the full fee if the session isn't cancelled at least 24 hours ahead of time.

Obviously, emergencies can happen. In that case, it is up to you on how to handle it. Just make sure that there is an understanding relating to cancellations when you first talk to the client.

Kids seem to get colds and the flu a lot, so if a parent contacts me a couple hours before the session to let me know that their child is sick, I give them a free pass. Actually, I prefer that they cancel due to sickness, even if they let me know one minute before I leave to go see them, because I don't want to catch what they have and get sick.

17

HOMEWORK

There are two types of homework. First, there is the homework that is issued by the child's school. Then there is the homework that you give the child.

Often, you will be asked to help a child with homework from school. Make sure you understand what the requirements are for completion of the assignment. Also, make sure that the parent wants you to help the child with the homework.

I had one client who told me not to help her son with math homework, that he was supposed to do that on his own. She only wanted me to help him with his English homework.

Now for the other type of homework, the homework you assign to the students. I have found this to be very helpful for non-native speakers that need English tutoring. I usually ask them to read a book (a short book for elementary school students) then write a one to three page book report. On rare occasions, they don't have time or forget to do it. But most of the time, the parents have been after them to get it done.

This works out well because I generally give them a worksheet to work on at the beginning of the session, and while they are working on it, I go through the book report and correct it for spelling, grammar, punctuation, and other issues. This makes my time productive while the student is working.

18

GIVING REWARDS AND GIFTS

Rewards can be a powerful influence for a student. On occasion, I have offered pens, pencils, and erasers to students as rewards for completing a lot of work or doing well in a session.

Sometimes I tell them ahead of time, sometimes I don't. I often tell a student who is occasionally hyperactive that he or she will get a reward if they behave during the tutoring session, and that seems to work.

If you are thinking of giving candy to a child as a reward, which usually happens before and especially after Halloween, check with the parent first to get their approval. Also, think twice before giving candy to a student who has trouble staying on task.

My advice is to avoid giving candy altogether.

In regards to gifts, I have given them to students who I have been working with for a long time, generally around the holidays, or end of school year.

The gifts are usually folders, notebooks, pens, and pencils.

There is one more type of reward I give to elementary students. With every worksheet I give them to work on, I write a star on the top after they are done, no matter how many mistakes they have made. I have also given them stickers. It may not seem like a lot to you, but it means a lot to the child.

19

TIME WASTERS

Speaking of making productive use of your time, you may at some point run into a client who takes excessive advantage of your time. I call them time wasters.

When I tutor a student for the first time, I usually spend some time after the session talking to the parent about what areas the student appears to be weak in and areas that need concentration. I also find out what things the student should work on. This time is important, even if you are not paid for the five or ten minutes of discussion time.

But after the first session, a one or two minute update to the parent is appropriate. For example, "He mixes his past tense and present tense in the book report. I explained to him how he needs to keep everything consistent in the past tense. We will work on that next week."

However, I had one client who would spend 15 to 20 minutes after EVERY session going over every worksheet, line by line, and turning to his child, saying "Why did you make this mistake?" and "Why did you make that mistake?" I couldn't leave because the client hadn't paid me yet.

But to add insult to injury, by the time the client was finished reviewing everything, he still hadn't written out the check to me, even though he had a whole hour to do so while the child was being tutored.

What was worse was that it took the client five minutes to write out the check. First, he would fill in the date, then he would ask me "Are you going to cover prepositions next week?" Then he would fill in the dollar amount, and ask if I would cover past participles. The questions would continue as each part of the check was being filled in.

After experiencing this several times, I finally put an end to it by telling him that I had to leave at 5:00pm sharp (the time the session normally ends) for another appointment. (My appointment was with myself to go home and have dinner.)

By the way, this same client asked me once if I would give his son an extra ten minutes of tutoring for free. My answer was a simple, "No."

20

TUTORING ADULTS

Tutoring for adults is not much different than teaching children. Adults tend to cancel and reschedule appointments more often, however, due to their busy lives.

Often a non-native speaker will want tutoring to improve their reading, writing, and speaking skills. They especially want to learn idioms.

Sometimes, a non-native speaker has to write a lot of reports for business, and needs help with them, especially in the area of grammar.

Other adults looking for tutoring include such skills as basic computer usage, Microsoft Excel, and Microsoft Word. (I have tutored all three, at a fairly high hourly rate, $50 to $150 per hour.) If you are proficient in several applications, make sure you include all of them in your advertising. Or if you are working through an agency, make sure that they are aware of all your skills.

The more obscure the subject you are tutoring, the higher you can charge.

Tutor Dominus

21

TUTORING COLLEGE STUDENTS

College students are always looking for help with various subjects that they may be studying for their undergraduate degree.

Those that are going on to graduate school need tutors to help them with preparation for the GMAT, LSAT, and GRE exams. If you can score in the 99th percentile on any of these exams, you can be very well paid.

For example, at the time this book is being written, a company called Manhattan Prep in San Francisco is hiring tutors for the GMAT at $116 per hour, according to a recent Craigslist ad.

Another company called Testcrackers in Santa Clara, California, advertised that it is paying $120 per hour for teaching GMAT and GRE preparation.

22

TUTORING ONLINE

Tutoring online will be the wave of the future, but it is already happening now in a big way. There are many schools that connect Americans up with students from various countries around the world, especially China.

But even many students in the U.S. prefer being taught through Skype from American tutors instead of in-person sessions.

The advantages to tutoring online are numerous:

1. You don't have to drive anywhere.
2. The client doesn't have to drive anywhere (e.g. the library)
3. Less carbon footprint.
4. Spend less money on gas.
5. Frees up more of your time for additional tutoring or just fun time.
6. You can provide services to clients around the world, not just locally.

Skype is the most common tool to do online tutoring. There are other alternatives, such as:

Google Hangouts
Appear.in (no registrations or downloads)
Talky.io (No downloads, signup, or payment required)
OOVOO.com
Viber.com
WeChat (web.wechat.com)
Jitsi.org

Tutoring online will generally require that you have a scanner and strong bandwidth. I use a lot of worksheets with my clients, so what I do is scan the worksheets (if I don't yet have them stored electronically), and save them in a folder for each particular client.

Then as we are going through the session, I either email or send through Skype the next worksheet that I want them to work on. I don't email them all ahead of time, as I like the idea of spontaneity. When they are done with the worksheet, I have them scan or take a picture and email it back to me, which I then print.

I make any corrections, then either show them on Skype or I scan the corrected worksheet and send it back to them. It is a fairly simple process once you get the hang of it.

23

BOOKKEEPING

If you are running your computer business on your own, you need to keep thorough records for tax purposes. I am not an accountant or tax preparer, and you should contact your tax specialist for additional information, but based on what the IRS allows, you should keep track of all of the following:

Mileage to all tutoring sessions

All auto expenses including gas, new tires, oil changes, tolls, etc. (your tax preparer can explain the difference comparing these expenses to mileage)

Computer

Printer

Ink

Paper

Pens

Pencils

Erasers

Tutoring books

Software (e.g. Microsoft Word)

Any gifts you may give your students

Possibly part or all of your tax preparation fee

Possibly part or all of your cell phone bill

Anything else that you use directly for tutoring

Make sure you save your receipts and keep them organized. You probably won't be incorporated so you will be filing what is called a Schedule C with your 1040 tax return. This schedule is for self-employed people.

Talk to your accountant for more details.

24

MARKETING

Getting your name out there may be the hardest part of your tutoring business. It would be helpful to have your own website or blog or both.

There are several resources that allow you to set up your own web site and blog for free, including:

Blogger
Wix
Weebly
Wordpress.com
Wordpress.org

I have used Blogger (owned by Google), Wix, and Wordpress. I have found blogger the easiest to set up a blog and Wix for setting up a website, with a blog included.

You should be aware that the free feature of Wix has a small ad for the company. You can pay for premium services, and not have the ad appear.

Your website should include a lot of keywords in the description of your services. Examples include the following:

Instructor
Educator

Teach
Teacher
Tutor
Tutoring
Education
Training
Learning

You should also include the specific areas that you tutor. If you tutor math, examples might be:
Math
Mathematics
Arithmetic
Adding
Subtracting
Multiplying
Dividing
Algebra
Geometry
Trigonometry
Calculus

But most important of all, you need to include the city you live in and all the surrounding cities and towns. Even the names of communities and neighborhoods. Include all the areas you are willing to drive to. I set my maximum limit to a one hour drive in commute traffic.

As a matter of fact, the name of your website should include your primary city or town. For example, if you live in Anytown, try to register the domain name Anytowntutoring.com or Tutoringanytown.com. If XYZtown is next to Anytown, try to register XYZtowntutoring.com as an additional domain name, then have that domain point to Anytowntutoring dot com. Have your domain registrar help you with that.

This way, your web site should show up near the top of the list on search engines if anyone types in "Anytown tutoring" looking for a local tutor.

In regards to business cards, I've rarely passed them out. One time, I just wrote my name, email, and phone number on a scrap of paper.

However, the cost of business cards has dropped so low even free, that it's probably worth getting 250 or 500 of them. Vistaprint is fairly inexpensive. Try this link which usually has big discounts:

Vistaprint.com/free

I have found that tri-fold brochures are a waste of money, even if they are cheap. Prospective customers usually toss them, but they always keep the business card.

Tutor Dominus

25

FREE WORKSHEETS & SAMPLE TESTS

There are plenty of free online resources for tutors, whether it is for elementary students, middle school students, or high school for PSAT, SAT and ACT preparation. The appendix has a list of various web sites that provide these resources.

The worksheets cover everything from math, to reading, to grammar, to vocabulary. There are plenty of grade appropriate spelling lists. There are even worksheets for students to practice printing and cursive writing.

The many SAT worksheets include reading, writing and language, math-no calculator, math-calculator, and essay. The ACT worksheets include English, math, reading, science, and writing. All of these worksheets provide answer keys and most provide discussions for each right and wrong answer, making it easier for you to help explain to the student the reasoning behind the answers.

In order to keep the student's attention, I like to mix up the worksheets during the tutoring session. In other words, if I am teaching an elementary student, I might have them work on a grammar worksheet for ten minutes, then a math worksheet for another ten minutes, then a spelling test after that and so on. If I am working with a high school student on ACT preparation, I give an English practice test first, then a math test, then reading, and finally science. I have found that concentrating on one area for more than 15 or 20 minutes will cause the student to lose interest and become bored.

There is one point that I need to cover regarding the "free" factor of these worksheets. The way that they web site generate income, besides advertising, is generally through the sale of workbooks which provide additional worksheets that can be utilized with your tutoring sessions. In order to support these companies that provide these free resources, I strongly recommend that you purchase some of their materials to help these businesses out financially.

In addition to the free worksheets, you can always create your own. It may take a bit of your time, but once they are created, you can use them over and over.

Here is an example of a worksheet that I use as a story starter for elementary and middle school students:

I have found that this type of worksheet can be used for first graders all the way up to sixth graders. It is a great exercise to have them practice their creative writing skills, and the spelling, grammar, and punctuation. A larger example of this worksheet can be found in the Appendix.

As you can see, it is a very simple worksheet to create. In this particular example, it was a matter of coming up with a couple of story starter sentences, pasting in a public domain picture from Wikipedia, and putting in lines.

Once this worksheet was done, it was easy to make additional worksheets. I just did a Save As, came up with a couple more sentences about an additional topic, such as riding on an airplane, or going to a restaurant, and typing those in over the former sentences, then finding an appropriate picture. In less than a minute, a new worksheet.

Obviously, creating a grammar worksheet would take a lot more time and work so using one of the worksheets available on the Internet would be more appropriate. The same thing goes for the ACT and SAT rep. No need to reinvent the wheel.

Tutor Dominus

FREE RESOURCES THAT CAN PUT MONEY IN YOUR POCKET

The following resources are websites which can provide you with all sorts of information relating to schools, agencies, and advertising web sites for tutors.

In addition, sources of free worksheets and sample tests are also included.

ADVERTISING YOUR TUTORING SERVICES

MyTutorList free classifieds
http://www.mytutorlist.com

Teachers.net free tutoring services ad
https://teachers.net/classifieds/tutorsavailable/submit.html

Tower of English free classifieds
http://www.towerofenglish.com/Post-Ad.html

Find a Tutor
http://www.tutor-ads.com

HappyTutors (fee-based listing)
http://www.happytutors.com/RegisterAsaTutor/

Tutor Agent Language Tutor Classifieds
http://tutoragent.com

CraigsList
http://Craigslist.org

Upwork
https://www.upwork.com

ONLINE SCHOOLS

ESL Jobs World
http://www.esljobsworld.com

Italki
https://www.italki.com/teacher/apply

LOIEnglish
http://www.skypeenglishclasses.com

TutorABC
http://recruit.tutorabc.com/program/index.asp

VIPKID
https://t.vipkid.com.cn/opportunity

Verbling
https://www.verbling.com/teach

Kukuspeak
http://www.kukuspeak.com/English.html

Myngle
http://www.myngle.com

Blabmate has a list of online English schools
http://www.eslbase.com/schools/online

DaDaABC
https://www.dadaabc.com/teacher/jobsummary

LARGE TUTORING ORGANIZATIONS

These are some of the largest tutoring companies in the United States.

Sylvan Learning
http://sylvanlearning.com

Kuman
http://kumon.com

Huntington Learning Center
http://huntingtonhelps.com

Mathnasium
http://mathnasium.com

TUTORING AGENCIES

There are numerous tutoring agencies. Here are just a few. By the way, there are plenty of local and regional tutoring agencies. Google "tutor" and a major city in your area to find them.

Wyzant
http://wyzant.com

Elite Home Tutoring
http://elitehometutoring.com

Tutor.com
http://tutor.com

TutorMe
http://tutorme.com

Skooli
http://skooli.com

Chegg Tutors
https://www.chegg.com/tutors/

FREE WORKSHEETS FOR ELEMENTARY & MIDDLE SCHOOL STUDENTS

K5Learning
http://k5learning.com/free-worksheets-for-kids

K12Reader
http://k12reader.com

Tlsbooks
http://tlsbooks.com

BigActivities
http://bigactivities.com

TurtleDiary
http://turtlediary.com/worksheets.html

SuperTeacherWorksheets
http://superteacherworksheets.com

Englishlinx
http://englishlinx.com

EReadingWorksheets
http://ereadingworksheets.com

HaveFunTeaching
http://havefunteaching.com

FREE WORKSHEETS FOR SAT AND ACT PREPARATION

CollegeBoard
https://collegereadiness.collegeboard.org/sat/practice/full-length-practice-tests

ACT.org
https://www.act.org/content/dam/act/unsecured/documents/Preparing-for-the-ACT.pdf

Reason Prep
http://reasonprep.com/practice-sats/

Prep Scholar - ACT
http://blog.prepscholar.com/printable-act-practice-tests-5-free

Prep Scholar - SAT
http://blog.prepscholar.com/printable-sat-practice-tests-4-free-official-tests

Free Test Online
http://www.free-test-online.com/act-test/act-worksheets

Free Mathematics Tutorials
http://www.analyzemath.com/ACT_SAT_practice.html

PowerScore
https://www.powerscore.com/sat/help/content_practic e_tests.cfm

Magoosh
https://magoosh.com/hs/sat/2016/printable-resources-sat-prep/

EricTheRed
http://www.erikthered.com/tutor/practice.html

InstructorWeb
https://www.instructorweb.com/lesson/satvocabularyle ss.asp

WORKSHEETS FOR ESL

Lanternfish (BogglesWorldESL)
http://bogglesworldesl.com

ONLINE TUTORING PLATFORMS

Skype
Google Hangouts
Appear.in (no registrations or downloads)
Talky.io (No downloads, signup, or payment required)
OOVOO.com
Viber.com
WeChat (web.wechat.com)
Jitsi.org
Zoom.us
WebEx

SOURCES OF PAY LEVELS

http://Findtutorsnearme.com

http://CraigsList.org

ESL MEETING PLACE RESOURCE

DavesESLCafe
http://www.daveseslcafe.com

PRIMARY LIST OF KEYWORDS

These are words that you must use in your website, along with all related words for the topics you teach.

Instructor
Educator
Teach
Teacher
Tutor
Tutoring
Education
Training
Learning

Sample Exercise

Name _____

I was at the park and when I looked up in the sky, I saw a UFO. The UFO landed on the ground and then

_____

_____

_____

_____

_____

_____

_____

_____

_____

_____

_____

_____

NEW CLIENT INFORMATION FORM

Name of student _____

Age: _____   Grade _____

Name of Mother _____

Mother's Phone _____

Mother's Email _____

Name of Father _____

Father's Phone _____

Father's Email _____

Address: _____

Subjects to be taught:

_____

_____

Any challenges (ESL, ADHD, etc.):

_____

Schedule:
Day(s) of the week: _____

Time of day: _____

Other information:

Tutor Dominus

THANK YOU

Thank you for reading this book. Now is your chance to put much of this information to use. As a special thanks for reading the book, I am offering free tips for tutors. You can get them by going to the following link:

http://tutoryourway.com

Also, it would really help me out to get your feedback. Your honest review of the book would be appreciated. You can post a review at Amazon by using the following quick link:

http://amzn.to/2uz6biZ

www.ingramcontent.com/pod-product-compliance
Lightning Source LLC
Chambersburg PA
CBHW071255170526
45165CB00003B/1360